D0997159

Wild Shropshire

Photography by Mark Sisson

Words by Sarah Gibson

This book has been produced to
celebrate the 50th anniversary of
Shropshire Wildlife Trust

Wild Shropshire has been generously funded by
the Jean Jackson Charitable Trust
and supported by a bequest from Mary Hignett
to the Oswestry branch of Shropshire Wildlife Trust

Foreword

By Bill Oddie

Most people have heard of Shropshire, but not many know where it is. They may even be familiar with Shropshire place names – such as The Long Mynd, Stiperstones, and Wenlock Edge – but they don't know what they actually look like. For those who live in, appreciate, study, and enjoy Shropshire's wild places and wildlife this book is a celebration. To those who don't yet know the county's many and varied delights, it may well be a revelation. It is also a lavishly illustrated 50th birthday card.

Any photographic collection of landscapes, birds, flowers and animals is certain to be impressive, but it can be rather dull. Not when Mark Sisson is behind the camera. Fellow photographers will appreciate the technical skills – defocused backgrounds, soft focused flowers, off-centre framing, and subtlety of shape, shadow and light. Pictures like these don't just happen by accident. This is the beauty of nature enhanced by human creativity. This is art!

Such images are timeless, but alas the landscape is not. Inevitably, over the years, some wild places have diminished or been lost, and with them some of the wildlife. These days the work of The Wildlife Trusts and other organisations is not so much conservation as creation and management. This is nature enhanced by human ingenuity and effort. Thanks indeed to those who have given their support in the form of time, expertise, enthusiasm and money, including funding this book.

Oh by the way, Shropshire is west of Birmingham, just before you get to the border with Wales. There is heathland, woodland, bogs, mires, meres, streams, outcrops and valleys, history and geology, and wildlife-rich canals. All in one small county that most people have heard of, but don't know where it is. Until now.

Wild Shropshire

The 50th anniversary of Shropshire Wildlife Trust is a moment to celebrate. It is also a time to reflect on the varying fortunes of Shropshire's wildlife, to explore the landscape and all that lives in it and to consider what the future may bring.

Ever since people first sharpened axes from stones and carved tools from deer antlers, they have shaped the landscape; cutting down trees, grazing their animals and clearing ground to build their homes. Yet for thousands of years wildness survived in marvellous variety and abundance, often despite the best efforts of people to control it.

Agricultural conformity

Nature, ever opportunistic, has been hugely successful at exploiting the open clearings and cultivated land that people have striven to create. But over the last half century or so, technological advances in equipment and agro-chemicals have resulted in a farming industry so efficient that it has all but wiped out the rich variety of wild plants from our grasslands and the lovely arable weeds from our crops, while marshes and bogs have been drained into agricultural conformity.

Quite suddenly, within our life-time and that of our parents, wild nature has come under threat. While individual species, such as birds of prey, moles and polecats have been persecuted for centuries, never before has the landscape itself been so drastically controlled. Progress (and what a dangerous word that now seems) is finally triumphing over nature.

Pioneers

Luckily, there have been people who stood up to this tide of destruction. Often derided as sandal-wearing tree-huggers, nature conservationists swiftly became respected through their sound scientific arguments and as a result, a force to be reckoned with. It is thanks to the passion and determination of those early pioneers that some of the very best wild places were saved from the onslaughts of change and protected as nature reserves. As well as securing beautiful places for the future, the pioneers campaigned. When the north Shropshire peat bogs – the Mosses at Fenn's, Whixall and Bettisfield – were threatened with industrial-scale commercial extraction, it was Shropshire Wildlife Trust that led the battle to save them (Ellesmere Branch deserve particular credit for their role in the campaign) – and won.

Over the last half century the perception of nature conservation has changed. This movement – for such it is – has the wide support of the public. Almost everyone agrees that it is a good and necessary thing. Ideas that once seemed cranky have become mainstream. Agri-environment schemes now pay farmers to include the needs of wildlife in their operations. Their availability is limited, but they exist.

Shropshire Wildlife Trust has changed too. It has grown substantially and is supported by more than 10,000 members, all of them wanting to do their bit to help the county they love. It has around 30 members of staff and is assisted in many ways by hundreds of volunteers.

A living landscape

Shropshire Wildlife Trust's vision has grown too. While nature reserves remain a crucial part of its activity, the Trust is also seeking ways of connecting wild places over huge areas by working with other landowners and partners, stitching fragmented landscapes back together.

Immense challenges are looming for wild places everywhere: climate change, economic constraints, urban development, inappropriate management and even neglect all pose continuing threats. Wild places and wildlife need to be connected to thrive; when fragmented they become vulnerable.

This is an exciting vision and we can all play a part in making happen. Everyone with a garden or a hanging basket can do something to encourage wildlife. And every donation, membership subscription or legacy to Shropshire Wildlife Trust makes a difference; each day given by volunteers looking after wild places helps mend the web of nature reaching across the county and beyond.

This book sets out to show the extraordinary beauty and diversity of wildlife still present in Shropshire and to tell the stories of its survival. Hopefully it will inspire many more people to join us in our determined efforts to give wild places a future.

Veronica Cossons
President, Shropshire Wildlife Trust

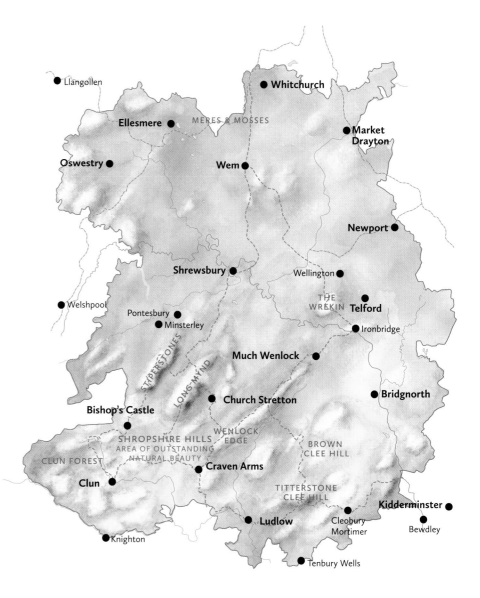

A Photographer's Perspective

I'm genuinely lucky and hugely appreciative to be able to earn my living out of photographing the natural world. My work takes me around the country and overseas with considerable regularity but I am equally as happy, probably more so on occasion, spending time in my own backyard unearthing photographic opportunities there.

This book has been almost two years in the making, but many more than that in terms of the content and has provided me with plenty of local encounters – hours spent sitting in my home town's canal interacting with the local mute swan cygnets, trying to tempt a robin to come close to my remotely operated camera in the middle of a particularly freezing winter day, dawn patrols in the local stream to find a roosting banded demoiselle damselfly in just the right place and even taking to the air to capture the amazing meanders of the River Severn that I simply couldn't do justice from any land-based angle.

The team at Shropshire Wildlife Trust has provided the framework and partnership needed to enable this book to be produced;

they also frequently provided that essential final contact that made things possible image-wise and the right motivation when certain species were proving particularly challenging in others. It's been a privilege to work with them to bring this project together as part of their 50th anniversary celebrations.

My work is almost all pure pleasure (well it is for me anyway) but it's the graft of individuals, many on a voluntary basis, at a local and community based level through Shropshire Wildlife Trust that allows much of the diversity this county enjoys to remain in place. I hope this collection of images that looks to celebrate the wildlife and some of the wild places it inhabits inspires you too in some way and encourages you to seek out the arrays of shape, colour, form and substance of nature that can be found by the enquiring and patient eye, whilst at the same time reflecting on its presence as well as its future prospects. Enjoy Wild Shropshire.

Mark Sisson

Wetlands & Waterways

Water tumbles down into Shropshire from the Welsh hills, the River Severn meandering through the county for 73 miles. Most of the time it is a tranquil presence in the landscape; occasionally it is transformed into a mighty torrent, bringing floods to fields and havoc to towns.

The Severn and its tributaries are brimming with life; it was along these rivers that otters from Wales returned to Shropshire in the 1990s after their brush with extinction thirty years earlier, the disastrous result of organochlorine pesticide use. Wildlife Trusts along the entire length of the river are now working together on projects to reduce the rapid run-off of rainfall, alleviate flooding and encourage wildlife-friendly farming.

Twelve thousand years ago north Shropshire was buried under hundreds of metres of ice. Slowly it melted, leaving behind deep holes that filled with water, a wetland mosaic that developed into the uniquely marvellous meres and mosses. Numerous fragments of this ancient wilderness survive, beautiful meres rustling with dragonflies, hundreds of ponds and ragged looking bogs where cotton-grass blows in the breeze and enormous spiders walk on water.

Shropshire's network of canals is a reminder of its industrial past; the highways that transported coal to Shrewsbury and the insatiable foundries of Ironbridge, and lime quarried from the Oswestry hills to fertilise the fields of outlying agricultural districts. Today these quiet backwaters are favoured by swans, kingfishers and moorhens and enjoyed by people out for a gentle stroll.

Man-made wetlands can be spectacularly successful for wildlife. The large, shallow pools at Wood Lane nature reserve, near Ellesmere are a haven for wetland birds, the result of landscape restoration by Tudor Griffiths Group on the site of worked out sand and gravel pits.

Lastly, let's not forget the streams and ditches that bubble along somewhere close to us all. Water voles can still be found in some; many other creatures and wild plants swim, float, travel and root themselves along these quiet waterways.

▶ Aerial view of the Severn meanders near Buildwas;
an ox-bow lake beckons in future centuries.

▲ A bullhead, also known as miller's thumb. They live in stony-bottomed streams and rivers, feeding at dusk on insects, larvae and fish fry. They in turn are food for kingfishers, herons, dippers, pike and trout.

◀ Heron at The Mere, Ellesmere. Herons first bred on the lake's Moscow Island 40 years ago. The island was constructed in 1812, the year Napoleon invaded Moscow.

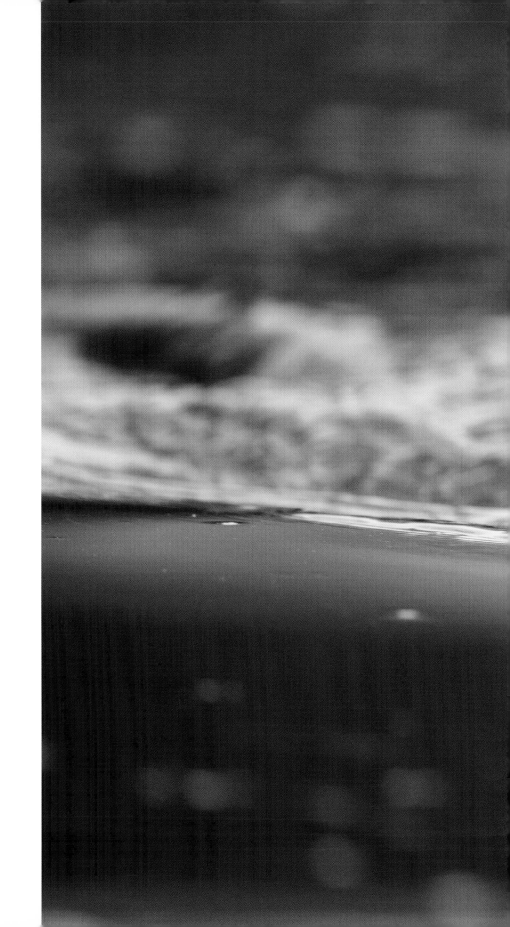

Otters underwent a catastrophic decline in the 1950s and 60s as a
result of toxic pesticides, with populations throughout Britain and
Europe devastated. Brought close to extinction, otters have now
reappeared in every county in England, thanks to improvements in
river quality and tighter pesticide controls.

Immortalised in the Wind in the Willows as Ratty, the water vole used to be a familiar creature of streams, rivers and ditches. The deliberate release of American mink from mink farms and their subsequent colonisation of waterways dealt a massive blow to these delightful creatures, which have disappeared from 95% of their former territories. The Whitchurch area remains a stronghold for water voles in Shropshire, thanks in no small part to the activity of the local water vole group.

Male reed buntings often sing from the top of vegetation. In recent years, this striking-looking wetland bird has started appearing in town gardens to feed in winter.

A mute swan, watchful at rest.

A stroll along a stream is always enlivened by the sight of a dipper bobbing up and down on a boulder, sometimes plunging into the water to catch food.

Wigeon often overwinter on flooded fields.

The Severn in flood along the Powys border.

The history of peat cutting in the north Shropshire mosses is evident from the air. Domestic hand cutting of peat on Whixall Moss is seen in the foreground with the more regular mechanised commercial peat cuttings of Fenn's Moss in the background, both re-wetted by Natural England and the Countryside Council for Wales since 1991.

A series of pools retains the watery character at Brown Moss, once an oozing peat bog. Drainage, peat cutting and thirsty trees have dried it out and the moss is gradually becoming woodland.

The wild expanse of Whixall Moss offers good winter hunting for the short-eared owl, often seen hunting by day over bogs and marshes.

The silky seed-plumes of common cotton-grass abound on the Shropshire mosses.

Raft spiders live in boggy pools, one of the largest spider species in Britain and a relative of the tarantula. It was once believed they used their silk to bind leaves together to float down streams, hence their name.

27

When little ringed plover first appeared in a wet field restored from a worked-out sand and gravel pit near Ellesmere, local birdwatchers came up with an idea. They approached Tudor Griffiths Group, the site owners, and persuaded them to make the most of the land's soggy qualities and create a shallow wetland. The project has been a spectacular success with thousands of wading birds dropping by on spring and autumn migrations and more than 180 species recorded. A pair of little ringed plover breeds here every year.

The banded demoiselle is often seen in summer along slow-flowing,
muddy-bottomed rivers such as the Severn.

Southern marsh
orchid at Sweeney
Fen nature reserve.

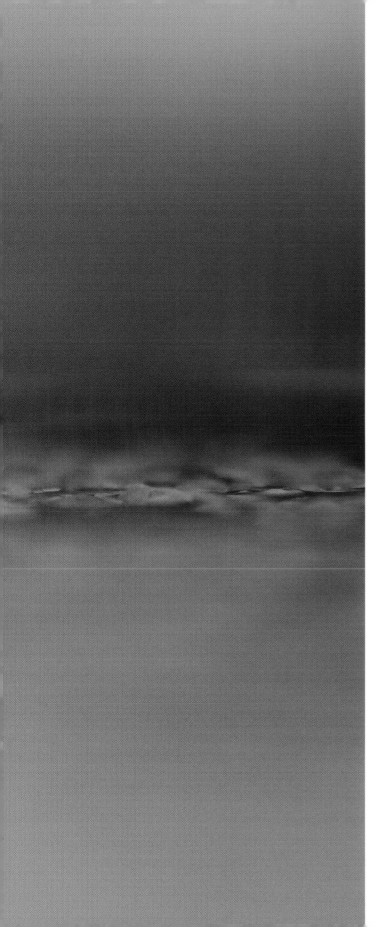

Grass snakes are strong swimmers but also spend much time basking on the edge of woods and fields. They live chiefly on a diet of frogs, toads and newts.

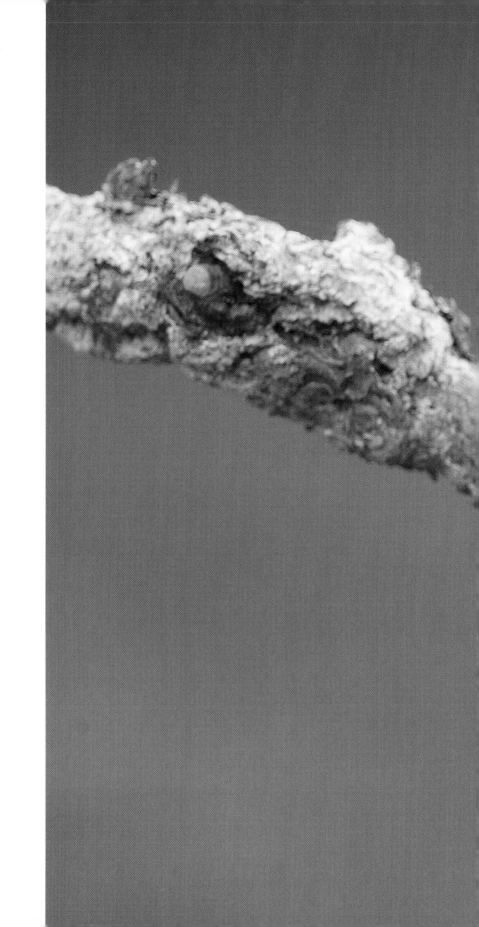

The kingfisher's beauty has brought it trouble over the centuries. In the Victorian era ladies wore its feathers in their hats, while thousands were caught, killed and preserved in glass domes to ornament parlours and drawing rooms. Today they are enjoyed in their element, glimpsed as a flash of brilliant blue over river or lake.

Uplands

Sixty years ago a new use was found for Britain's uplands. National policy to grow our own timber targeted the country's least agriculturally productive areas for conifer plantations. The Stiperstones, one of Shropshire's wildest places, with its jagged, quartzite tors and heathland, would soon be cloaked in the uniform dark green of Norway spruce.

Fortunately, a large tract of surviving heath was saved as a national nature reserve. By the 1990s the conifers were ready to fell and the Forestry Commission had changed its planting strategy. A partnership of local organisations, including Shropshire Wildlife Trust and Natural England, embarked on an ambitious scheme to remove the conifers and restore the heathland. A devastated landscape emerged when the trees were felled, the ground like a muddy battlefield. Soon though, a lively community effort resulted in local people planting thousands of heather plants; sacks of seed were sown and now the heather and whinberry are back, along with skylarks, meadow pipits and grasshoppers.

Few conifers were ever planted on The Long Mynd, but here too wildlife has had problems. EU payments in the last part of the 20th century encouraged commoners to graze a great many sheep, which quietly munched this enormous Site of Special Scientific Interest bald. Thankfully, the system has now changed, resulting in fewer sheep and the gradual recovery of this beautiful range of hills.

There are more than 50 Iron Age hillforts in Shropshire, the most familiar being The Wrekin. Old Oswestry, Bury Ditches and Titterstone Clee are particularly impressive; all of them are wonderfully atmospheric, providing a link back to the lives of people nearly 3,000 years ago.

The limestone hills around Oswestry are one of the most botanically-rich areas of the county. Numerous orchid species flourish in old quarries and commons, along with aromatic herbs such as thyme and marjoram, common rockrose and devil's bit scabious. Such variety of plants makes it an excellent place for butterflies, moths and other insects and all the birds and bats that feed on them.

Making a living from hill farming has never been easy and the future will be challenging. Even wild landscapes need farmers. Without grazing the newly recovered heathland on The Stiperstones would slowly revert to woodland.

▶ Heather at Cranberry Rock on The Stiperstones.

From The Hollies nature reserve on The Stiperstones,
to Lawn Hill and The Wrekin.

Remnant
hedge near The
Stiperstones.

Sunlit valley on the Long Mynd near Ashes Hollow.

Bury Ditches is one of the most tranquil places in Shropshire. For several decades it was shrouded in conifers, but a storm blew many of them down in the 1970s; then the Forestry Commission felled the remainder, revealing the magnificent Iron Age hillfort.

An ancient grove of holly trees on The Stiperstones is a rare survivor of the once widespread practice of holly pollarding. Branches of the trees were cut for winter cattle fodder (the leaves are surprisingly nutritious) and this regular pruning has reinvigorated the trees over centuries.

A characterful hawthorn at Cardingmill Valley on the Long Mynd.

Common grasshopper juvenile. They can leap 20 times the length of their body; their astonishing muscle power is equalled only by the shell-closing snap of the clam.

The star-like flowers of bog asphodel are seen in late summer on boggy ground such as Catherton Common in the Clee hills. Following Shropshire Wildlife Trust's purchase of the common in 2009, a survey revealed this wild heathland as a national stronghold for the common lizard.

Adders, along with lizards, other reptiles and toads, have experienced a
sharp decline in numbers. Persecution used to be their main problem,
today it is habitat loss and fragmentation.

Red grouse breed on The Stiperstones and Long Mynd. The cock was vividly described by the naturalist WH Hudson as resembling 'a figure cut in some hard dark red stone... red gritstone or ironstone... or better still, deep-red serpentine, veined and mottled with black'.

Persecution during the 19th century led to the extinction of ravens in Shropshire in 1884. Over the last 90 years they have slowly recovered, most rapidly over the last 20 years. There are now more than 250 pairs breeding across the county.

Rhos Fiddle nature reserve, in the uplands above Clun, is one of the last outposts for breeding snipe. Traditional hardy breeds such as Highland cattle, graze the heath and grassland, ensuring the vegetation stays in good shape.

The wheatear is a bird of stony, upland pastures. The 1950s devastation of the rabbit population had a knock-on impact on this upright little bird, as the closely-grazed swards where it fed disappeared and the supply of abandoned rabbit burrows used for nesting holes collapsed. Unlike the rabbit, the wheatear's numbers have never fully recovered.

The wren is the UK's commonest breeding bird, seen everywhere from wild uplands to parks and gardens.

Meadow pipits are one of the cuckoo's main hosts in upland areas and adult birds are frequently taken by buzzards and ravens.

The UK's smallest bird of prey, the merlin may occasionally be seen on the Long Mynd.

The old quarries of the Oswestry hills have restored themselves naturally with a rich mosaic of vegetation: Bee orchid.

Grizzled skipper

Farmland

Never have people been so successful at producing food as they are today. Technological advances have infiltrated every aspect of agriculture from the development of chemical fertilisers and pesticides to new breeds of high yielding plants and livestock. Production levels are high and food is relatively cheap. But there is a hidden cost.

Industrialised farming has resulted in huge losses of landscape and wildlife; insect abundance and variety have crashed as a result of agricultural change and this has impacted drastically on many birds and other wild creatures. Nor has all progress been efficient. EU payments have encouraged the planting of crops in unsuitable places, such as flood plains, while sheep subsidies in the 1980s led to an explosion in flock sizes and serious overgrazing of pastures. Soil erosion and degradation is widespread.

Over recent decades agricultural aspirations have broadened and grants become available to redress specific environmental problems. Wetlands have been recreated, beetle banks built along the edges of fields and new hedges planted. These grants are a life-line to wildlife and in many cases to farmers themselves, yet economic austerity has cast a shadow of doubt over the future of these payments. But birds and butterflies are not a luxury to be sacrificed in times of hardship, they are evidence of a functioning environment.

Nature gives us many gifts that we take for granted, from pollination by bees and other insects to climate regulation, genetic resources, flood control and spiritual inspiration. Slowly, governments are starting to recognise the enormous economic contribution of nature to our lives; now what is needed is a strategy to protect and restore natural areas and connections between them. The demands on land have never been greater, but we ignore the role of nature in helping to deliver them at our peril.

▶ Rainbow over a harvested carrot field near Caynton.

Field trees add beauty and interest to the landscape. They often mark the line of former hedgerows.

Harrowing fields near The Wrekin, it is black-headed gulls that follow the
tractor for worms and insects, not lapwing flocks as in the past.

Villain or victim? The badger is blamed for many countryside problems, from a rise in bovine TB to a decline in hedgehogs.

The brown hare has grown much less common, but is still seen where land is less intensively managed.

First identified by Gilbert White in 1767, the harvest mouse was at that time much more abundant and frequently found in sheaves of corn and farmyard ricks. The introduction of reaping machines brought about a steep decline in its numbers. The discovery of a harvest mouse nest near Church Stretton in 2005 was the first sign of its presence in Shropshire in nearly 30 years.

Rabbits and rats thrive in the modern environment, their rapid breeding
cycles and adaptability giving them an edge over more specialised animals.

Industrialised farmland has a certain minimalist beauty,
unfortunately accompanied by minimal wildlife.

Once a common sight around the fringes of our fields, the grey
partridge has declined steeply over the last 25 years.

Hedgerows criss-cross the landscape, providing nesting sites, a harvest of berries and nuts and natural corridors for insects, birds and small mammals. Karl Liebscher is a master hedge-layer, keeping a traditional skill alive. Sloes are still widely collected in Shropshire, a marvellous addition to gin.

The greenfinch is a seed-eater who scours the fields and hedgebanks for food.

Hips and haws are a vital source of food in winter for many birds including redwing.

◄ This magnificent splash of poppies in a field of rapeseed, near Edgmond, has appeared only once in the last 15 years. Poppy seeds can lie dormant for decades, making a sudden dramatic appearance when conditions are right.

Some 98% of England's traditionally managed hay meadows have vanished from the landscape over the last 50 years. Melverley Meadows, a Shropshire Wildlife Trust nature reserve near Whitchurch, is one of the few survivors. With its heath-spotted orchids, ragged robin and numerous other flowers, it is a haven for butterflies including large skippers.

Spotted flycatchers make a brief summer appearance in the UK, raising a single brood before their long migration south. They regularly return to the same nest sites around old farm buildings, but their numbers have dropped steadily, partly as a result of disturbance in their wintering grounds or along migration routes.

In past centuries swallows used to nest in chimneys, earning them the name of chimney swallow. Today they are known as barn swallows, but as farm buildings are redeveloped for housing, they are often found in porches, sheds, garages and even warehouses. Kestrels also like to nest in barns and readily take to nest boxes.

Myxomatosis wiped out 90% of the rabbit population in the 1950s, a crushing blow for the common buzzard as rabbits form a major part of its diet. Since then both rabbits and buzzards have made a spectacular comeback and this magnificent bird's shrill cry is now heard over field, village and town.

▶ A sky full of lapwing is a sight remembered from childhood, all too rarely seen today.

Town & Garden

Gardens are where most people enjoy their closest contact with nature and where they can most directly and easily do something to help wildlife. Across the UK there are a million acres of gardens, great swathes of marvellous green space.

Passionate wildlife gardeners dig ponds, plant hedges and trees, make compost heaps and log piles, grow gorgeous nectar-rich plants beloved by butterflies and make leaf heaps for hibernating ladybirds. They also quite deliberately avoid being over-tidy, to encourage beetles, spiders and a vast array of creepy crawly creatures to live in their gardens.

Bird feeding is hugely popular; peanuts, sunflower seeds and a host of specialist mixes are hung out in tubes and heaped on bird tables, bringing birds within a few feet of our windows. More kinds of birds than ever are visiting gardens, with goldfinch now one of the top garden bird visitors and bullfinch regularly sighted too. Not all garden birds have been winners though, song thrush and house sparrow have declined markedly in recent years. Keeping gardens chemical-free and abundantly full of nature may give them a chance to recover.

Gardens connect wildlife to other green places such as parks, churchyards, railway lines and roadside verges and ultimately to the countryside beyond. Such green networks are vital to keep wildlife populations healthy; they also contribute to the quality of life in the urban environment. Places for children to play, teenagers to idle about in and the rest of us to stroll along and watch the seasons unfold are essential to refresh our spirits.

Development pressure on green space in towns is huge, especially in Telford and Shrewsbury. People need homes and houses must be built, but a visionary approach is needed that will give recognition and protection to the most special wild places and the links between them. Shropshire Wildlife Trust campaigns hard to make this happen.

▶ This aerial shot of Wellington reveals how extensive town gardens often are; a patchwork of green space stitched to the countryside beyond.

A bee-friendly garden is easy to establish if you choose the right plants. Teasels have an additional bonus: after bees have pollinated the flowers, goldfinches come along and eat the seeds.

The rise in garden bird feeding over the last 50 years has done wonders for old familiars such as blue tits, while the acrobatic long-tailed tit has more recently ventured in from the countryside, much to the delight of all who feed and watch them.

Feathers fluffed out, this robin is working hard to survive the freezing temperatures. Knee deep in snow, heat loss is minimised by special scales on its legs and feet.

The great spotted woodpecker is a garden favourite despite its appetite for small birds' eggs and nestlings. Blue tits, great tits and even house martins are regularly preyed on.

This seven-spot ladybird is the gardener's friend, a voracious eater of greenfly.

It took several days waist-deep in Newport canal to gain the confidence of this cygnet, much to the amusement of passers-by.

Coots are strict and aggressive parents, occasionally killing a chick if it steps out of line. They are one of our most abundant urban water birds.

Great crested grebes are regularly seen in the pools of Telford Town Park and other urban lakes. Their feathers were widely used in ladies' hats in the Victorian era, which almost resulted in their extinction. A campaign against their collection led to a group of women founding the RSPB in Manchester in 1889.

The great crested newt has wielded considerable power over the last few decades; its protected status blocking or altering many development proposals. Its legal protection is vital though; the loss of farm ponds over the last half century has seriously reduced its abundance. The old canal in Shrewsbury is home to a particularly dense population and the region as a whole is one of its strongholds internationally.

Introduced from north America in the late 19th century, the grey squirrel has displaced our native red squirrels and is a serious predator of woodland birds' eggs and nestlings. It also successfully competes for food such as nuts, seeds and berries.

Hedgehogs are declining but gardens are a stronghold; by leaving piles of leaves, not being too tidy and making sure small gaps in fences allow gardens to link together, people can help them.

Bees in urban and suburban settings have a richer, healthier diet than bees in farmland settings. While modern agriculture relies on the honeybee for crop pollination, its system of monocultures conspires against a thriving bee population.

British households throw away vast amounts of food and food packaging. This rotting food and waste contributes the equivalent of 20 million tons of carbon dioxide a year to the atmosphere, but gulls make a good living from our throwaway habits.

Berry-bearing trees and bushes planted in shopping centre car parks
provide winter food for the occasional influx of waxwings from
Scandinavia and blackbirds.

Snow has brought traffic to a halt, the moorhen is on the move.

Toads make hazardous journeys over roads and railway lines back to their breeding pools in early spring. Garden ponds are of great value to them and their appetite for slugs and snails is of great value to gardeners.

Getting close
to nature is an
essential part of
childhood.

Feeding geese at Priorslee Flash.

Woodland

From a distance, the north Shropshire plain appears to be covered in trees. This is, of course, an illusion created by the network of hedges and hedgerow trees between the highly cultivated arable fields. Centuries of forest clearance have shrunk Shropshire's woodland cover to a tiny percentage of the landscape. But the ancient woods that do survive, such as the oak dingles of south Shropshire, are wonderfully interesting.

Others are on steep hills, such as Wenlock Edge. Here you can feel a link with the earth's ancient past; the ground beneath your feet was once under the sea, an ancient barrier reef, formed 400 million years ago south of the equator. Herb Paris, sanicle and sweet woodruff grow, thriving on the fossilised remains of corals and other shelled creatures.

People lived and worked in woods for thousands of years. Charcoal burning around the Wrekin reached a peak at the beginning of the industrial revolution. The remains of old charcoal hearths are still visible; this industry, which powered the furnaces of Ironbridge, ended here less than 100 years ago.

Charcoal burning ensured the continuous renewal of woods through coppicing. Glades would be opened up every 15 years or so by felling trees which then sprang back afresh. As the ancient art of coppicing dwindled, woods grew dark and overgrown; violets, primroses and bluebells were shaded out.

Luckily, Shropshire Wildlife Trust and other conservation minded organisations have led a revival in coppicing, helping to keep our woods alive.

The woods of the Oswestry hills are marked by industry too. Numerous ruined limekilns can be found, trailing with ivy, held together by the roots of trees. Spindle bushes, with their flaming orange and pink berries, colonise well in these old, limestone quarries; greater butterfly orchids, early purples and twayblade reveal their mysterious flowers.

Conifers have been planted in many of the county's native woods. Some, such as those at Hope Valley nature reserve, have later been taken out, giving the oaks and bluebells a second chance. At Haughmond Hill, Forestry Commission planting thankfully spared some wonderful veteran trees and heathland; the open rides of Mortimer Forest and the Wyre Forest are good for butterflies, wild flowers and fungi.

▶ Nothing is more breathtakingly lovely than a wood in spring awash with bluebells.

Woods along the west Shropshire border have a distinctively Welsh character, with wind-blasted sessile oaks clinging to steep valleys. These trees at Lurkenhope Wood nature reserve, near Knighton, are host to numerous kinds of lichens and mosses.

Hoar frost in Chetwynd Deer Park.

Silver birch in autumn and winter.

135

Catching sight of a roosting tawny owl by day is a delight. More often they are glimpsed in flight at dusk or we hear their familiar "twit-twoo" calls to each other.

Summer visiting pied flycatchers and common redstarts raise their young
in insect-rich woodlands. They nest in tree holes and are increasingly
reliant on bird boxes.

Treecreepers often roost in the bark of large, old trees, pecking out hollows to shelter from freezing temperatures and rain.

With three toes at the front of its foot and one at the back, the nuthatch is fantastically agile, walking straight down and across trees, rooting out food with its rapier-like bill.

The hazel dormouse sleeps for seven months of the year and is seldom seen except by specially trained nestbox checkers who monitor their presence in Shropshire's ancient woods. This one snored loudly as it slowly woke from the torpor of hibernation.

143

Also known as fitchew, foumart and foul marten, on account of its famous stink, the pole cat reached the brink of extinction after relentless persecution by gamekeepers in the 19th century. Today it has widely re-established itself in Wales and central England and has even moved into towns, where it eats rats and scavenges as urban foxes do.

Once hunted by kings and the nobility, fallow deer have spread far beyond the bounds of the royal hunting forests to which they were introduced in medieval times. Their numbers today pose a significant threat to woodland regeneration, careful management is required to keep deer populations healthy and woods alive.

Clockwise from top left: common dog-violet, lesser
celandine, herb Paris and wild garlic.

Wood anemone with nymph.

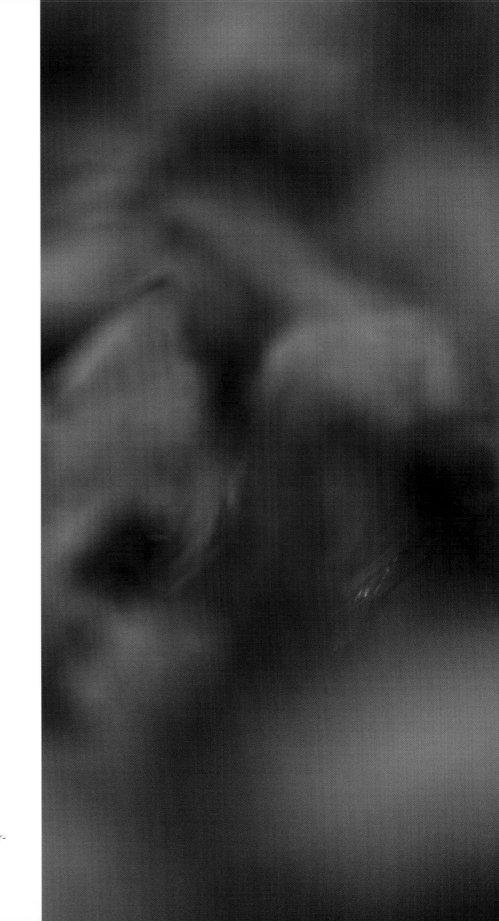

The gem-studded puffball is also known as the devil's snuffbox, as a powder-like shower of spores takes to the air when it ripens and bursts open.

Fly agaric and translucent porcelain fungi glow in a shaft of sunlight.

Shropshire Wildlife Trust's volunteers spend many winter days coppicing and managing woodland. Selective felling of trees lets in sunlight, encouraging spring flowers and butterflies.

Domino, a Welsh cob, tushes timber the traditional way
from The Ercall nature reserve, near Wellington.

155

The Ercall's woods are considered ancient, but in comparison to the 550 million year old rocks they are decidedly new.

This isolated woodland in a field near Clun, symbolises the problems for wildlife of habitat fragmentation.

Old & New

A mighty stretch of the imagination is needed to visualise the extraordinary changes undergone by the earth over millions of years. We get hold of this past in glimpses: fossils embedded in our hills provide hard evidence that this bit of land we call Shropshire emerged from the sea; woolly mammoth skeletons, found in a quarry near Condover, confirm that these huge elephants roamed the landscape during the Ice Age.

Change has always been part of life on earth but it has speeded up dramatically over the last 100 years. Technology has given humans the upper hand over nature, while population pressures and lifestyle expectations are increasing the demand on land to deliver food, housing and industry.

Climate change is with us already and will inevitably lead to more disruption in the natural world. There will be winners as well as losers; bluebells may disappear but little egrets and Dartford warblers will arrive.

There is a growing realisation of our dependence of nature, reflected in government statements, if not yet in strategies backed up with finance. This rising awareness gives us hope. The conservation story shows that with a lot of will and relatively small amounts of money, we can make a big difference. With vision, our landscape can accommodate thriving wild places and wildlife. Nature is dynamic, endlessly renewing herself and seizing opportunities. It is up to us to make sure she gets her chance.

▶ The red kite is a bird with a future. As with many birds of prey, it was heavily persecuted during the 19th century but has slowly recovered during the last 100 years. Since 2006 more than 70 young have been raised in Shropshire.

Species have disappeared from the county over thousands of years, bears probably being the first big predators to be wiped out here by humans. Wolves survived a few more centuries; in Shropshire a commission was issued in 1281 to destroy every wolf in the county.

Red squirrels disappeared from Shropshire in the late 1950s; the introduction of the American grey was a major cause of its destruction.

The decline of farmland birds such as corn bunting is the
direct result of intensive modern agriculture.

Whitcliffe Common, Ludlow used to be a hotspot for hawfinches. The population across the UK has crashed over the last 20 years.

Pearl-bordered fritillaries have suffered the consequences of dark, neglected woodlands over recent decades. They need sunny glades and open paths with a plentiful supply of violets for their caterpillars to eat. Targeted conservation work on nature reserves can make a real difference to their future.

Apple blossom: the grubbing out of old orchards made uneconomic by cheap imports has dealt a blow to many kinds of wildlife from bees to lichens. The good news is that small-scale community orchards are springing up in towns and villages.

The last surviving colony of silver-studded blue butterflies in the Midlands can be found at Prees Heath Common near Whitchurch. Its survival is little short of miraculous, but restoration of the heath is gradually improving the fortunes of these isolated butterflies.

The consequences of climate change are hard to predict. Likely winners are little egrets, now regular breeders in the south of England and the marbled white butterfly. Watch out for these in Shropshire as the weather warms up.

▸ The magnificent osprey has returned to Wales to breed in recent years. How long before a pair nests in Shropshire?

Footnote

In the interests of integrity I think it's important to add as a footnote to this work that on grounds of practicality, a desire to minimise disturbance to very small local populations and in an attempt to deliver the visual experience that they warrant in this work, a small number of subjects represented in this book were photographed either outside the county or under controlled conditions.

Acknowledgements

I'd like to thank the following for their support in making this whole book and the images therein come to fruition.

John Hughes and Sarah Gibson at Shropshire Wildlife Trust who've been involved from day one and before.

Ellie Rothnie who provides a constant sounding board and keeps me on the commercial straight and narrow.

Mike Ashton for his support and expertise in producing a final design and style we're all happy with.

All of those landowners, farmers, volunteers and plenty of others too who've allowed me access to their land, fields, woods and properties to photograph some of the county's special wildlife that might be found there: too many to name individually but you know who you all are.

Last but by no means least, my wife Caroline and the rest of my family for putting up with my lifestyle and obsession with what I do in the name of work.

Mark Sisson

Winter sunset near Newport.